STECK-VAUGHN

Gateways™

Writer's Notebook

Program Authors

Action Learning Systems, Inc.

Robin Scarcella, Ph.D., Hector Rivera, Ph.D., and Mabel Rivera, Ph.D.
English Language Development

Isabel L. Beck, Ph.D. and Margaret McKeown, Ph.D.
Vocabulary

Penny Chiappe-Collins, Ph.D.
Decoding

HOUGHTON MIFFLIN HARCOURT
Supplemental Publishers

www.SteckVaughn.com
800-531-5015

Steck-Vaughn *Gateways, Writer's Notebook*

ISBN 10: 1-4190-5668-9
ISBN 13: 978-1-4190-5668-0

Writing Prompt: Narrative

Think About It

Think about a particular event in which you did something admirable. It could be something you did for a friend, a family member, or the community. It could be a time when you made a difference or used your talent in a helpful or respectful way.

Write About It

Write a narrative about a particular event in which you did something admirable. Write your narrative like a story. Include concrete sensory details that show the setting. Provide details that show what happened during the event and who was involved. Organize your narrative with a clear beginning, middle, and end. Be sure to describe this event in a way that will help readers see your actions as admirable.

{ **NARRATIVE CHECKLIST** }

- ☐ Read the prompt carefully and respond to all parts of the prompt.
- ☐ Organize the narrative with a beginning, middle, and end.
- ☐ Include concrete sensory details to describe the setting.
- ☐ Include details to describe the characters.
- ☐ Identify why the actions were admirable.
- ☐ Check for errors in grammar, spelling, and punctuation.

Topic Toss: Narrative

{ Admirable Event }

Narrative Sketch

Admirable Event: ___________________________________

____

Narrative Map

Characters

Main: _______________________

____

____

Others: _______________________

____

____

Setting

Where: _______________________

____

____

When: _______________________

____

____

Plot

BEGINNING

____

____

____

MIDDLE

____

____

____

____

END

Why was it admirable? _______________________

____

____

Completed Writing Frame: Narrative

Something Admirable

(a creative title that relates to your topic)

BEGINNING

When I think of something I did that was admirable, I think about when

my brother Ramón and I went to my grandparents house . This
(identify an incident in which you did something admirable)

happened *one morning when we drove to our grandparents house* . I will never
(describe the time or date)

forget this event because *I felt proud to help them* .
(explain the outcome of the specific event)

It started when *we drove there after it snowed* .
(describe the beginning)

I could see *snow and I could see more snow.* .
(describe the setting)

MIDDLE

I thought *we could never be able to shovel that much snow* .
(explain what you thought)

I said, " *we is just kids* ." Next, *Abuelita was glad we was there* .
(record something important you said)   (describe the middle)

I saw *Abuelita with the shovels* . I wondered
(describe what you saw)

if Ramón and I coud help them . Then, *I knew it would be hard work* .
(explain what you wondered)   (describe more of the middle)

" *Do you think we can do it? Ramón asked* ."
(record something important another main character said)

Completed Writing Frame: Narrative

END

Finally, _we stumble into the house_ . I will always remember
(record the ending)

they were happy that we helped them. I'm happy, too. .
(explain why you will remember this event)

I think this event is admirable because _Abuelita said she could_
(explain why it was admirable)

never have done such hard work . I learned _that helping others is admirable_ .
(explain what you learned)

If I were given the opportunity again, I would _do it again_ .
(explain what you would do)

Idea Workshop: Narrative

Read your narrative aloud to your reviewer. Then ask your reviewer the following question. Write your reviewer's response below.

What did you like most about my narrative?

____

____

____

Now give your narrative and your Writer's Notebook to your reviewer.

REVIEWER: ____________________________

1. What happened in the beginning? What happened in the middle? What happened in the end?

BEGINNING

____

____

MIDDLE

____

____

END

____

____

____

2. What concrete sensory details helped you to picture the setting of this narrative?

____

____

Idea Workshop: Narrative

3. Which details helped you to understand the characters in this narrative?

4. What makes the actions admirable?

5. After reading this narrative, what would you like to learn more about?

Editor's Workshop: Narrative

Read each sentence in your partner's narrative. Circle each subject and underline each verb. Find sentences that need to be edited for subject-verb agreement. Number the sentences on your partner's narrative that need to be edited. Write the corrections below.

REVIEWER: _______________________

Edited Sentences

1. ____

   ____

2. ____

   ____

3. ____

   ____

4. ____

   ____

5. ____

   ____

6. ____

   ____

Scoring Rubric: Narrative

Rate the following categories from your narrative on a scale of 1 through 4, with 4 being the most effective and 1 being ineffective. A rating of 0 means you did not attempt to include this feature in your narrative.

Feature	Rating				
I showed what happened in the beginning, middle, and end.	0	1	2	3	4
I described the setting by using concrete sensory details.	0	1	2	3	4
I described the characters.	0	1	2	3	4
I wrote my narrative like a story, including appropriate narrative strategies.	0	1	2	3	4
I included a variety of sentence types.	0	1	2	3	4
I corrected my writing for grammar, spelling, and punctuation.	0	1	2	3	4

When I write a narrative in the future, I plan to…

- ☐ revisit the narrative prompt while I'm writing.
- ☐ make sure that my narrative is organized with a clear beginning, middle, and end.
- ☐ describe the setting by using more concrete sensory details.
- ☐ describe my characters in greater detail.
- ☐ include a variety of sentence types.
- ☐ edit more carefully for correct grammar, spelling, and punctuation.
- ☐ ______________________

Writing Prompt: Narrative

Think About It

All of us know ordinary people whose actions make us admire them. These people could be friends, family members, or neighbors. Think about an ordinary person you admire and identify a particular incident in which this person did something admirable.

Write About It

Write a narrative about an event in which someone you know did something admirable. Write your narrative like a story. Include concrete sensory details that show the setting. Provide details that show what happened during the event and who was involved. Organize your writing with a clear beginning, middle, and end. Be sure to write about this event in a way that will help your readers see this person's actions as admirable.

{ NARRATIVE CHECKLIST }

- ☐ Read the prompt carefully and respond to all parts of the prompt.
- ☐ Organize the narrative with a beginning, middle, and end.
- ☐ Include concrete sensory details to describe the setting.
- ☐ Include details to describe the characters.
- ☐ Identify why this person and event are admirable.
- ☐ Check for errors in grammar, spelling, and punctuation.

Topic Toss: Narrative

{ Admirable Event }

Completed Narrative Sketch

Admirable Event: ____

____

Narrative Map: Writing

Admirable Event: ____

____

Characters

Main: ____________________________________

____

Others: ____________________________________

____

Setting

Where: ____________________________________

____

When: ____________________________________

____

Plot

BEGINNING

____

____

MIDDLE

____

____

____

MIDDLE

____

____

____

END

Why was it admirable? ____________________________

____

____

Completed Writing Frame: Narrative

Sheila the Firefighter

(add a title that relates to your topic)

BEGINNING

One day or night ___there was a huge fire down the street___.
(describe the beginning)

___No one knows how it started. It is scary___ . ___The neighbors___
(describe the beginning)   (describe who was there)

___were outside trying to stay cool. When they saw smoke, they called the___
(describe who was there)

___firefighters. But my neighbor Sheila came to help___ .

___The fire was really big and it lasted all night.___
(describe the setting)

___It looked like a really dangerous fire___
(describe the setting)

MIDDLE

Then, ___she saved some people___ .
(explain why this person is admirable)

___Someone yeled "Fire!" and someone else screamed "Help."___
(state something important someone said)

Then, ___people were runing out of the apartment building. We could see the___
(describe the middle)

___fire burning We heard the siren and a fire truck came soon. It wuz crazy!___ .

After that, ___I see Sheila jump out of a fire truck___ . ___She had all her gear on an I___
(describe the middle)   (add more details)

Completed Writing Frame: Narrative

MIDDLE

knew was her cuz I seen Sheilas name.

(describe the middle)

I sees Sheila came out with a kid and a couple of other kids. They were messy but OK.

(describe what you saw)

Surprisingly, some people were crying and some are seeing burned out stuff.

(describe what surprised you)

Finally, it wuz really cool but Im glad the fire was out. I will always remember

(describe the ending)

END

Sheila because shes really brave. This incident is important because

(explain why you will remember this person and event)

I seen how hard fire fighters work an how they save people.

(explain why it is important)

If I could be more like Sheila I would be more brave.

(explain how you could be more like this person)

Idea Workshop: Narrative

Read your narrative aloud to your reviewer. Then ask your reviewer the following question. Write your reviewer's response below.

What did you like best about this narrative?

____

____

____

Now give your narrative and your Writer's Notebook to your reviewer.

REVIEWER: ______________________________

Answer the following questions about your partner's narrative.

1. What happened in the beginning? What happened in the middle? What happened in the end?

BEGINNING

____

____

MIDDLE

____

____

END

____

____

____

2. What concrete sensory details show the setting of this narrative?

____

____

Idea Workshop: Narrative

3. What details helped you to understand the characters in this narrative?

4. What makes this event admirable?

5. After reading this narrative, what would you like to learn more about?

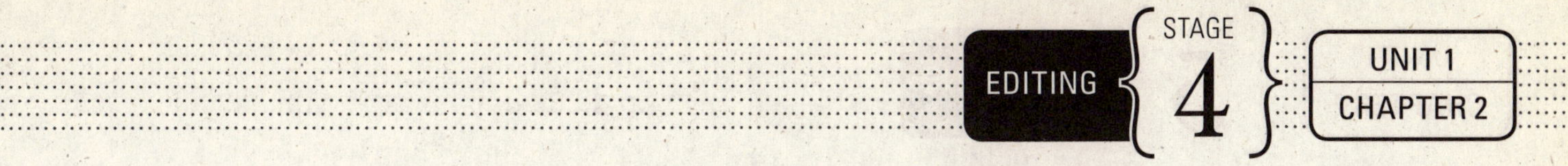

Editor's Workshop: Narrative

Read each sentence in your partner's narrative, and circle every verb. Find sentences in your partner's narrative that need to be edited for verb tense. Number the sentences on your partner's narrative. Write the corrections below.

{ **REVIEWER:** _______________________ }

Edited Sentences

1. ____

2. ____

3. ____

4. ____

5. ____

6. ____

Scoring Rubric: Narrative

Rate the following categories from your narrative on a scale of 1 through 4, with 4 being the most effective and 1 being ineffective. A rating of 0 means you did not attempt to include this feature in your narrative.

Feature	Rating				
I showed what happened in the beginning, middle, and end.	0	1	2	3	4
I described the setting by using concrete sensory details.	0	1	2	3	4
I described the characters.	0	1	2	3	4
I wrote my narrative like a story, including appropriate narrative strategies.	0	1	2	3	4
I included a variety of sentence types.	0	1	2	3	4
I corrected my writing for grammar, spelling, and punctuation.	0	1	2	3	4

When I write a narrative in the future, I plan to…

☐ revisit the narrative prompt while I'm writing.

☐ make sure that my narrative is organized with a clear beginning, middle, and end.

☐ describe the setting by using more concrete sensory details.

☐ describe my characters in greater detail.

☐ include a variety of sentence types.

☐ edit more carefully for correct grammar, spelling, and punctuation.

☐ ____

Writing Prompt: Narrative

Think About It

Think of a person you have read or heard about who has done something admirable. This person could be someone you read about in a book, saw on television or in the movies, or heard stories about. Think about what this person has accomplished and how these accomplishments have impacted the world.

Write About It

Write a narrative about someone you have seen, read, or heard about who did something admirable. Write your narrative like a story. Include concrete sensory details that show setting. Provide details that show what happened during the event and who was involved. Organize your writing with a clear beginning, middle, and end. Be sure to write about this event so your readers see this person's actions as admirable.

{ **NARRATIVE CHECKLIST** }

☐ Be sure to read the prompt carefully and look at all parts of the prompt.

☐ Organize the narrative with a beginning, middle, and end.

☐ Include concrete sensory details to describe the setting.

☐ Provide details to describe the characters.

☐ Identify why this person was admirable.

☐ Check for errors in grammar, spelling, and punctuation.

Topic Toss

{ *Admirable Events* }

Narrative Sketch

Admirable Event: ____

Narrative Map: Writing

Characters

Main: _______________________________

____

Others: _______________________________

____

Setting

Place: _______________________________

____

____

Time: _______________________________

____

Plot

BEGINNING
MIDDLE   MIDDLE   MIDDLE   MIDDLE
END

____

____

____

____

____

____

____

____

____

Why is this person admirable? _______________________________

____

Completed Writing Frame: Narrative

César Chávez is an Admirable Person

(a creative title that relates to your topic)

BEGINNING

I admire César Chávez. Chávez had many accomplishments in his life. Chávez was

a farm worker. Chavez organized a union. Farm workers needed Chavez's help for better

working conditions.

MIDDLE

Cesar Chavez got many honors. The president gave them a medal. He has a stamp

and parks and stuff named after and his birthday is a state holiday. Because of all this he

is a hero.

MIDDLE

Chavez planned a march of workers. Chavez wanted people to understand. He got a

small group of people to walk the farther they got the bigger the group grew. They started

in Delano. 75 people walking to Sacramento. By the time they reached Sacramento over

10,000. Many of the marches yelled like "Strike" and "Long live our cuase" in spanish.

Completed Writing Frame: Narrative

MIDDLE

He learned that many Mexican-Americans were not treated fair. His family was poor he had to work in the hot fields. He worked long hours for low pay. he started a union to fight for condishuns and pay for the workers. Chavez thought it was important to not fight. He learned this from Gandhi and Martin Luther King.

END

People around the country started to understand farm workers. Thousands of people were in the crowd. Chavez met with the land owners and the farm workers had triumph. He was happy that the land owners racted by agreeing to improve conditions for the workers.

Idea Workshop: Narrative

Read your narrative aloud to your reviewer. Then ask your reviewer the following question. Write your reviewer's response below.

What did you like best about this narrative?

____

____

____

Now give your narrative and your Writer's Notebook to your reviewer.

{ **REVIEWER:** _______________________ }

Answer the following questions about your partner's narrative.

1. What happened in the beginning? What happened in the middle? What happened in the end?

BEGINNING · MIDDLE · END

____

____

____

____

____

____

____

2. What concrete sensory details show the setting of this narrative?

____

____

____

Idea Workshop: Narrative

3. What details helped you to understand the characters in this narrative?

4. What makes this event admirable?

5. After reading this narrative, what would you like to learn more about?

Editor's Workshop

Read each sentence in your partner's narrative. Determine whether the correct pronoun was used or if a pronoun could be used in place of a noun. You will also look for places where pronouns are missing. Number the sentences on your partner's narrative. Write the corrections below.

REVIEWER: _______________________

Edited Sentences

1. _______________________
   ____

2. _______________________
   ____

3. _______________________
   ____

4. _______________________
   ____

5. _______________________
   ____

6. _______________________
   ____

Scoring Rubric: Narrative

Rate the following categories from your narrative on a scale of 1 through 4, with 4 being the most effective and 1 being ineffective. A rating of 0 means you did not attempt to include this feature in your narrative.

Feature	Rating				
I showed what happened in the beginning, middle, and end.	0	1	2	3	4
I described the setting by using concrete sensory details.	0	1	2	3	4
I described the characters.	0	1	2	3	4
I wrote my narrative like a story, including appropriate narrative strategies.	0	1	2	3	4
I included a variety of sentence types.	0	1	2	3	4
I corrected my writing for grammar, spelling, and punctuation.	0	1	2	3	4

When I write a narrative in the future, I plan to…

- ☐ revisit the narrative prompt while I'm writing.
- ☐ make sure that my narrative is organized with a clear beginning, middle, and end.
- ☐ describe the setting by using more concrete sensory details.
- ☐ describe my characters in greater detail.
- ☐ include a variety of sentence types.
- ☐ edit more carefully for correct grammar, spelling, and punctuation.
- ☐ ____

Writing Prompt: Persuasive Letter

Think About It

Each year the government spends millions of dollars on space exploration. Even though this amount is only one percent of total spending, some people feel that this money would be better spent in other areas, such as education, the environment, or the military. Think about how you think the money should be spent.

Write About It

Write a persuasive letter to the President of the United States about how you think the money should be spent. State your position clearly and include important evidence that supports your position. Organize your writing with a strong introduction, body, and conclusion. Identify possible reader concerns and address them. Remember, convince your reader that your position is the best one.

{ **PERSUASIVE CHECKLIST** }

- ☐ Read the prompt carefully and respond to all parts of the prompt.
- ☐ State your position clearly.
- ☐ Support your position with important evidence (details and examples).
- ☐ Organize your writing with a strong introduction, body, and conclusion.
- ☐ Address possible concerns that your reader might have.
- ☐ Check for errors in grammar, spelling, and punctuation.

Topic Toss

{ What should the government spend more money on? }

Position Organizer

Topic: How should the government spend its money?

Position: The government should spend its money on _______________.

Reasons	Evidence	Concerns
☐	• •	
☐	• •	
☐	• •	

Evidence Organizer: Persuasive Letter

Topic: How should the government spend its money?

Position: The government should spend its money on _________________

because ____

____

____ .

Topic Sentence 1: The government should spend its money on

_____________________ because _______________________________

____ .

{ EVIDENCE }

Evidence Organizer: Persuasive Letter

Topic Sentence 2: Some people say that _______________________

____ .

{ EVIDENCE }

However, ____

____ .

Completed Writing Frame: Persuasive Letter

<u>september</u>   <u>16</u> , <u>2009</u>
(Month)   (Day)   (Year)

HEADING

Dear Mr. President:

INTRODUCTION

Is the government spending too much money on space exploration? Many

people wonder if ___*it is too much*___ . I think the money would be best spent
(state a common thought)

___*on space exploration*___ . There are two important reasons why the government
(state area)

BODY

should spend its money on ___*space exploration*___ .
(state area)

Money should be spent on ___*space*___ because it will ___*keep*___
(state area)

___*problems from happening*___ . We could ___*have a picture of the universe*___ so
(state main reason why)   (provide detail)

that we could ___*learn from the astronauts*___ . If we ___*explore space*___ ,
(identify benefit)   (provide detail)

society will ___*learn*___ . ___*The research*___ would help ___*NASA*___
(provide reward)   (record thing, object, or idea)   (provide detail)

by ___*keeping them from having to rthink their ideas all the time*___ .
(provide reward)

Some people think that ___*the government should not spend money*___ ,
(state argument against your position)

Completed Writing Frame: Persuasive Letter

BODY

but they couldn't be more wrong. If _the money should be_
(provide detail)

spent on things like education or the millitary, then _these important topics would_
(state result)

never be learned about. Since _we might not be able to live on earth_
(state result)

it would be unwise to _not make it safe and don't send astronauts in space_.
(provide detail)

CONCLUSION

Government spending on _Exploration_ will benefit us in the
(state area)

future. When we think about _space exploration_ we know the government
(provide detail)

should help us _______________. It is for these reasons that I believe
(state area)

the government should spend money for astronauts to keep problems from happening.
(record main reason)

If we are to have _opportunities to explore space safety_,
(state type of condition)

we need to _______________.
(write closing statement)

CLOSING

Sincerely,

J.T. Romero
(Signature: first and last name)

J.T. Romero
(Print first and last name)

Idea Workshop

Read your persuasive letter aloud to your partner. After you read your letter, ask your partner the following question:

What did you like best about my persuasive letter?

____

____

____

Give your persuasive letter and Writer's Notebook to your partner. Answer the following questions about your partner's persuasive letter.

{ **REVIEWER:** _________________________ }

Read your partner's persuasive letter, then write your answers to the questions below.

1. What is my position?

____

____

____

2. What evidence did I include to support my position?

____

____

____

____

____

Idea Workshop

3. How did I address reader concerns?

4. What could I do to improve my letter?

Editor's Workshop

Read each sentence in your partner's persuasive letter. Find sentences that can be edited to create compound subjects and compound verbs. Number the sentences on the persuasive letter. Write the corrections below.

REVIEWER: _______________________________

Edited Sentences

1. ____

____

2. ____

____

3. ____

____

4. ____

____

5. ____

____

6. ____

____

Scoring Rubric: Persuasive Letter

Rate the following categories from your persuasive letter on a scale of one through four, with four being the most effective and one being ineffective. A rating of zero means you did not attempt to include this feature in your persuasive letter.

Feature	Rating				
I stated a position clearly.	0	1	2	3	4
I supported my position with relevant evidence.	0	1	2	3	4
I organized my writing with a strong introduction, body, and conclusion.	0	1	2	3	4
I addressed possible reader concerns.	0	1	2	3	4
I followed the format of a letter.	0	1	2	3	4
I included a variety of sentence types.	0	1	2	3	4
I corrected my writing for grammar, spelling, and punctuation.	0	1	2	3	4

When I write a persuasive letter in the future, I plan to . . .

- ☐ revisit the persuasive prompt while I'm writing.
- ☐ make sure that my persuasive letter clearly states a position.
- ☐ provide relevant evidence and effectively organize the writing.
- ☐ convincingly address the readers' concerns.
- ☐ follow the format of a letter.
- ☐ include a variety of sentence types.
- ☐ edit more carefully for correct grammar, spelling, and punctuation.
- ☐ ______________________________

Writing Prompt: Persuasive Letter

Think About It

In Chapter 1, we read about benefits and drawbacks of using animals as astronauts in the space program. Animals are sent to space so that humans can learn how space travel affects living beings. Often, these animals are put at risk. Some people think it is better to send animals to space because it reduces possible risk to humans. Other people disagree. What do you think about sending animals to space?

Write About It

Write a persuasive letter to NASA about whether animal astronauts should be used in the space program. State your position clearly and include important evidence that supports your position. Organize your writing with a clear introduction, body, and conclusion. Identify possible reader concerns and address them. Be sure to convince your reader that your position is the best one.

{ PERSUASIVE LETTER CHECKLIST }

- ☐ Read the prompt carefully and address all parts of the prompt.
- ☐ State your position clearly.
- ☐ Support your position with important evidence (details and examples).
- ☐ Organize your writing with a strong introduction, body, and conclusion.
- ☐ Address possible concerns that your reader might have.
- ☐ Check for errors in grammar, spelling, and punctuation.

Topic Toss: Persuasive Letter

{ *Using animal astronauts in the space program* }

Position Organizer

Topic: Should animal astronauts be used in the space program?

Position: Animal astronauts _________________ be used in the space program.

Reasons	Evidence	Concern
☐	• •	
☐	• •	
☐	• •	

Evidence Organizer: Persuasive Letter

Topic: Should animal astronauts be used in the space program?

Position: Animal astronauts ______________ be used in the space program.

Topic Sentence 1: Animal astronauts ______________ be used in the

space program because ____.

{ **EVIDENCE** }

Topic Sentence 2: Another reason why animal astronauts ______________

be used in the space program is ________________________________.

{ **EVIDENCE** }

Evidence Organizer: Persuasive Letter

Topic Sentence 3: Some people say _______________________________

____.

{ EVIDENCE }

However, ____.

Completed Writing Frame: Persuasive Letter

HEADING

November _______ 30 _______ , 2009 _______
(Month)   (Day)   (Year)

____
(write salutation)

INTRODUCTION

Should we send animals into space ? Animals are sent to space, so we can learn
(pose question)

how space travel might affect humans. _Once they sent a monkey to space_ .
(describe what happens when animals are sent into space)

For example, _when the monkey was in space_, we learned _about weightlessnes_ .
(provide an example)   (explain what happened or what we learned)

I don't know if they should or not because _animals get hurt_ and
(state position)   (state reason 1)

learn about weightlessnes .
(state reason 2)

BODY

Sometimes bad things happened to animals that went into space . For example,
(restate reason 1 as a topic sentence)

one time a dog died when it went to space because it got too hot in the capsule. The
(provide evidence)

dog died only after about three hours .

Scientests have gotten a lot of information about weitlessness and now they know
(restate reason 2 as a topic sentence)

enough about how to use that for making space travel safe .

Completed Writing Frame: Persuasive Letter

BODY

For example, _like the millionaire_ (provide evidence) . In addition, _animals used in_ (provide evidence)

these experiments have died from suffocashun or exploshun (provide evidence) . These reasons

clearly support NASA _discontinuing_ (continuing/discontinuing) use of animals in the space program.

BODY

Many people believe that experimenting with animals is _good_ (insert reader concern) .

They argue that _we can learn a lot about space. Maybe people can travel to space_ (provide evidence)

and be safe becuz of the animals. Even if they die .

However, _it really isn't that fair to those exterordinary animals_ (address reader concern) .

NASA should _discontinue_ (continue/discontinue) the use of animals in the space program.

CONCLUSION

Even though _we learn a lot about space_ (restate reader concern) , it is important to _be fair to_ (restate your position)

the animals because _it is too dangerous for them, and that's not right_ (summarize your evidence)

because they could get hurt .

CLOSING

Sincerely,

Trang Lo
(signature: first and last name)

Idea Workshop: Persuasive Letter

Read your persuasive letter aloud to your partner. After you read your letter, ask your partner the following question:

What did you like best about my persuasive letter?

____

____

____

Give your persuasive letter and Writer's Notebook to your partner. Answer the following questions about your partner's persuasive letter.

{ **REVIEWER:** _________________________ }

Read your partner's persuasive letter, then write your answers to the questions below.

1. In one sentence, summarize my position.

____

____

____

2. What evidence did I include to support my position?

____

____

____

____

Idea Workshop: Persuasive Letter

3. How did I address reader concerns?

____

____

____

4. What could I do to improve my letter?

____

____

____

____

____

____

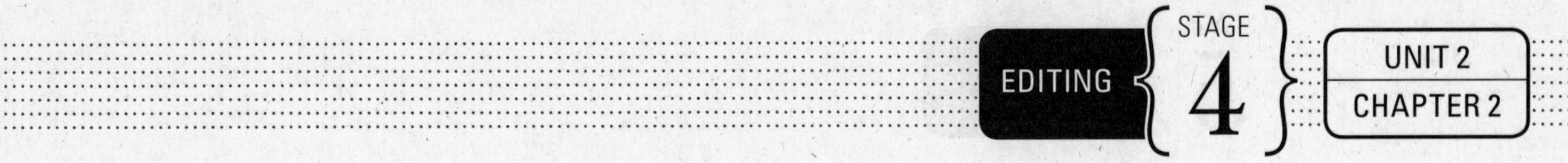

Editor's Workshop: Persuasive Letter

Read each sentence in your partner's persuasive letter. Find sentences in your partner's letter that can be combined and compound sentences that are missing commas or conjunctions. Number the sentences on your partner's letter. Write the corrections below.

REVIEWER: ______________________________

Edited Sentences

1. ____

____

2. ____

____

3. ____

____

4. ____

____

5. ____

____

6. ____

____

Scoring Rubric: Persuasive Letter

Rate the following categories from your persuasive letter on a scale of one through four, with four being the most effective and one being ineffective. A rating of zero means you did not attempt to include this feature in your persuasive letter.

Feature	Rating				
I stated a position clearly.	0	1	2	3	4
I supported my position with relevant evidence.	0	1	2	3	4
I organized my writing with a strong introduction, body, and conclusion.	0	1	2	3	4
I addressed possible reader concerns.	0	1	2	3	4
I followed the format of a letter.	0	1	2	3	4
I included a variety of sentence types.	0	1	2	3	4
I corrected my writing for grammar, spelling, and punctuation.	0	1	2	3	4

When I write a persuasive letter in the future, I plan to . . .

☐ revisit the persuasive prompt while I'm writing.

☐ make sure that my persuasive letter clearly states a position.

☐ provide relevant evidence and effectively organize the writing.

☐ convincingly address the readers' concerns.

☐ follow the format of a letter.

☐ include a variety of sentence types.

☐ edit more carefully for correct grammar, spelling, and punctuation.

☐ ____

Writing Prompt: Persuasive Letter

Think About It

Imagine being one of the first space tourists to vacation on a space station. A new company, *Space Travel Today,* is accepting applications for anyone who is interested in space travel vacations. *Space Travel Today* has asked people to write letters explaining why they deserve to travel in space. Thousands of people will apply, but only ten will be chosen. Think about if you would like to spend a year in space, or if you would like to nominate someone you know.

Write About It

Write a persuasive letter to *Space Travel Today* nominating yourself or someone you know to spend a year in space. Be sure to state your position clearly and include relevant evidence that supports your position. Organize your writing with a strong introduction, body, and conclusion. Identify and address possible reader concerns. Convince your reader that your position is the best one.

{ **PERSUASIVE CHECKLIST** }

When I write a persuasive letter in the future, I plan to . . .

- [ ] read the prompt carefully and respond to all parts of the prompt.
- [ ] state position clearly.
- [ ] provide important evidence.
- [ ] organize writing with a strong introduction, body, and conclusion.
- [ ] convincingly address reader concerns.
- [ ] include a variety of sentence types.
- [ ] edit more carefully for correct grammar, spelling, and punctuation.

Topic Toss: Persuasive Letter

{ Who deserves a space travel vacation? }

Position Organizer

Topic: Who deserves a space travel vacation?

Position: _________________ deserve(s) a space travel vacation.

Reasons	Evidence	Concern
☐	• • •	
☐	• • •	
☐	• • •	

Evidence Organizer: Persuasive Letter

Position: _________________ deserve(s) a space travel vacation.

Topic Sentence 1: _________________ should be chosen for a space travel vacation because _________________

____

{ **EVIDENCE** }

Topic Sentence 2: Another reason _________________ should be chosen for a space travel vacation is that _________________

_________________ .

{ **EVIDENCE** }

Evidence Organizer: Persuasive Letter

Topic Sentence 3: Some people think _______________________________

____.

{ **EVIDENCE** }

However, ____

____.

Completed Writing Frame: Persuasive Letter

month, day, year

To Whom It May Concern:

Shouldn't someone who deserves to travel to space be the person that is chose for

your space travel vacation? I have the perfect person for your trip. "a space survey was

conducted in 1993. Seventy percent of people questioned that they would go to space",

that is one of my teachers! My teacher, Mr. King, has always loved space and rockets .
(Position)

Some of you might think that a teacher is not the best person for the trip. If a
(Topic Sentence)

teacher was in space for a year, who would teach the class? Some kids need extra help in

science. And if all the teachers took trips like this one it would be hard, but Kang wrote

Olsen described to one group of students it was like camping. Mr. King would think a lot

about this problem, but would he still be the best person for a space vacation. .

The football field, Mr. King taught us about different kinds of rockets. We even built
(Topic Sentence 2)

Completed Writing Frame: Persuasive Letter

BODY

one. If it wasn't for Mr. King's excitemet and his knowledge we never would have learned

how to make the rockets. He told us how he wanted to be an astronaut when he was a boy.

He would be a fearles astronaut. Another reason why Mr. King is perfect is because he

loves to teach. We had to learn about the solar system, and made a model that had the

sun in it. One day the sun will turn into a black hole. Then all the planets will get sucked
(Topic Sentence 3)

BODY

into it. Including earth to. The sun is actually a star, and it is shrinking!

I also think that if Mr. King went to space, he would be able to do experiments. Like how

the sun is so big, you could fit thousands of earths in it, and other planets. Think about the

students who could watch him when he taught the lessons from space! That would be

CLOSING

good more kids than just those in my class. That is why Mr. King should be picked.

Sincerely,

Johnny Dough
(signature: first and last name)

Idea Workshop: Persuasive Letter

Read your persuasive letter aloud to your partner. After you read your letter, ask your partner the following question:

What did you like best about my persuasive letter?

Give your persuasive letter and Writer's Notebook to your partner. Answer the following questions about your partner's persuasive letter.

{ **REVIEWER:** }

Read your partner's persuasive letter, then write your answers to the questions below.

1. In one sentence, summarize my position.

2. What evidence did I include to support my position?

Idea Workshop: Persuasive Letter

3. How did I address reader concerns?

4. What could I do to improve my letter?

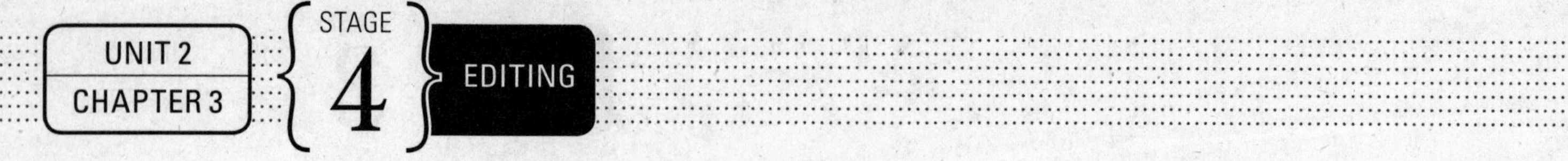

Editor's Workshop: Persuasive Letter

Read each sentence of your partner's persuasive letter. Find sentences in your partner's letter that can be edited for prepositional phrases. Number the sentence on your partner's letter. Write the corrections below.

{ **REVIEWER:** _________________________ }

Edited Sentences

1. ____
   ____

2. ____
   ____

3. ____
   ____

4. ____
   ____

5. ____
   ____

6. ____
   ____

Scoring Rubric: Persuasive Letter

Rate the following categories from your persuasive letter on a scale of one through four, with four being the most effective and one being ineffective. A rating of zero means you did not attempt to include this feature in your persuasive letter.

Feature	Rating				
I stated a position clearly.	0	1	2	3	4
I supported my position with relevant evidence.	0	1	2	3	4
I organized my writing with a strong introduction, body, and conclusion.	0	1	2	3	4
I addressed possible reader concerns.	0	1	2	3	4
I followed the format of a letter.	0	1	2	3	4
I included a variety of sentence types.	0	1	2	3	4
I corrected my writing for grammar, spelling, and punctuation.	0	1	2	3	4

When I write a persuasive letter in the future, I plan to . . .

- [ ] revisit the persuasive prompt while I'm writing.
- [ ] make sure that my persuasive letter clearly states a position.
- [ ] provide relevant evidence and effectively organize the writing.
- [ ] convincingly address the readers' concerns.
- [ ] follow the format of a letter.
- [ ] include a variety of sentence types.
- [ ] edit more carefully for correct grammar, spelling, and punctuation.
- [ ] ____

Writing Prompt: Response to Literature

Think About It

You have just read the trickster tale "The Fox and the Crow," and have been asked to write a character review of Crow for an internet bookstore. Throughout the story, we learn more and more about Crow as a character and how he is easy to fool. Think about how Crow acts, how he reacts to Fox, and what he says.

Write About It

Write a response to literature describing the character traits of Crow. Develop a thoughtful interpretation that explains why this character is easy to fool. Organize your writing with a clear introduction, body, and conclusion. Support your ideas with textual evidence.

{ **RESPONSE TO LITERATURE CHECKLIST** }

- [ ] Read the prompt carefully and respond to all parts of the prompt.
- [ ] Develop a thoughtful interpretation.
- [ ] Organize your writing with a strong introduction, body, and conclusion.
- [ ] Provide textual evidence from the text that supports your interpretation.
- [ ] Use words that are appropriate to your audience and purpose.
- [ ] Check for mistakes in grammar, spelling, and punctuation.

Topic Toss: Response to Literature

{ Description of Crow }

Character Log: Response to Literature

Text: ____

Character Name: ______________________________________

{ **What does the character look like?** }

{ **What does the character do?** }

{ **What does the character say?** }

{ **What do others say about the character?** }

Evidence Organizer: Response to Literature

Controlling Idea: __________ is easy to fool because he is __________ and __________ .

Topic Sentence 1: __________ is easy to fool because __________

__________ .

Textual Evidence

-
-
-
-
-

Commentary/Analysis

-
-
-
-
-

Evidence Organizer: Response to Literature

Topic Sentence 2: _____________ is also easy to fool because _____________

_____________.

Textual Evidence

-
-
-

Commentary/Analysis

-
-
-

Completed Writing Frame: Response to Literature

Crow is dirty and thinks he's great

(an interesting title that describes your essay)

INTRODUCTION

In trickster tales one character gets fooled by another. In the story

"   The Fox and the Crow   ,"   Crow   gets fooled
(identify title of the story)   (identify first character)

by   Fox   . We learn about   Crow   through his
(identify second character)   (identify first character)

thoughts, words, and actions.   Crow   is easy to fool because he is
                                       (identify first character)

          dirty   and   thinks he is great   .
(identify first trait of first character)   (identify second trait of first character)

BODY

          Crow   is easy to fool because   he is dirty
(identify first character)   (identify first trait of first character)

                                                  . At the beginning of the story,

          Crow has cheese in his mouth and Fox wants it.
(describe the situation, problem, or conflict)

          Fox tricks him into dropping the cheese
(describe what happens next)

Because of this,   Crow looses his chees   .
               (describe what the character does)

We also see that   Crow   is   dirty   when
               (identify first character)   (identify first trait)

Completed Writing Frame: Response to Literature

he shows his messy feathers .
(describe what second character does and/or says)

He is not very clean .
(describe what it shows about the first character)

Crow is also easy to fool because _he will_
(identify first character)   (identify second trait of first character)

be thinking he is way cool . _He showed off when he puffs his feathers_ .
                                         (describe how first character shows this trait)

If _he weren't so into hisself and_ were less _stuck on hisself_ ,
(identify first character)   (identify second character trait)

they wouldn't have lost the cheese .
(explain how the outcome would be different)

This would _make everybody mad at the trick_ .
(explain how it would show the first character's trait)

Crow is easy to fool, because _he out of tuch and a fool_ .
                                         (first and second character trait)

He open his beek and drop the cheese . By the end of the story,
(state again what happened in the story)

he gets reelly mad .
(explain what we learned about the first character being tricked)

BODY

CONCLUSION

Idea Workshop: Response to Literature

Read your response to literature aloud to your reviewer. Then ask your reviewer the following question. Write your reviewer's response below.

What did you like best about my response to literature?

____

____

____

Now give your response to literature and your Writer's Notebook to your reviewer.

{ **REVIEWER:** _______________________ }

1. How would you summarize my response to literature?

____

____

____

____

____

2. What is my controlling idea?

____

____

____

3. What evidence supports my controlling idea?

____

____

____

Idea Workshop: Response to Literature

4. Is there any evidence that needs to be taken out because it isn't important or it isn't from the text? If so, write this evidence below.

5. What ideas and evidence should be added to improve this response to literature?

Editor's Workshop: Response to Literature

Read each sentence of your partner's response to literature. Circle the verb in each sentence. Find sentences with regular or irregular verbs that need to be edited for present tense. Number the sentence on your partner's response to literature. Write the corrections below next to the same number.

{ **REVIEWER:** _______________________________ }

Edited Sentences

1. ____
____

2. ____
____

3. ____
____

4. ____
____

5. ____
____

6. ____
____

Scoring Rubric: Response to Literature

Rate the following categories from your response to literature on a scale of 1 through 4, with 4 being the most effective and 1 being ineffective. A rating of 0 means you did not attempt to include this feature in your response to literature.

Feature	Rating				
I established a controlling idea clearly.	0	1	2	3	4
I developed my topic with relevant evidence.	0	1	2	3	4
I showed an understanding of the text.	0	1	2	3	4
I organized my writing with a strong introduction, body, and conclusion.	0	1	2	3	4
I included a variety of sentence types.	0	1	2	3	4
I corrected my writing for grammar, spelling, and punctuation.	0	1	2	3	4

When I write a response to literature in the future, I plan to…

☐ revisit the response to literature prompt while I'm writing.

☐ make sure that my response to literature clearly establishes a controlling idea.

☐ provide relevant evidence.

☐ show an understanding of the text.

☐ effectively organize the writing.

☐ include a variety of sentence types.

☐ edit more carefully for correct grammar, spelling, and punctuation.

☐ ____

Writing Prompt: Response to Literature

Think About It

An animation company has said that whoever writes a winning comparison of two tricksters will win an all-day trip to their animation studios. Consider two characters you have read about and their interesting and unique traits. Think about the similarities and differences between their characteristics, motivations, and the results of their actions.

Write About It

Write a response to literature in which you discuss two tricksters. Compare and contrast the characters' similarities and differences. Develop a thoughtful interpretation that explains how their unique character traits help them to succeed.

Be sure to organize your writing with a clear introduction, body, and conclusion.

Support your ideas with textual evidence from the text.

{ **RESPONSE TO LITERATURE CHECKLIST** }

- [ ] Read the prompt carefully and respond to all parts of the prompt.
- [ ] Develop a thoughtful interpretation and position.
- [ ] Organize your writing with a strong introduction, body, and conclusion.
- [ ] Provide textual evidence that supports your interpretation.
- [ ] Use words that are appropriate to my audience and purpose.
- [ ] Check for mistakes in grammar, spelling, and punctuation.

Topic Toss

{ Description of tricksters }

Contrasting Character Log

Text: ____

{CHARACTER #1}

{CHARACTER #2}

{Similarities Between Characters}

Differences Between Characters With Regards To:

←···· ACTIONS ····→

←···· MOTIVES ····→

←···· APPEARANCES ····→

←···· CHARACTER TRAITS ····→

Evidence Organizer: Response to Literature

Controlling Idea: _________________ and _________________ are similar

because ____ but different because

____ .

{ Topic Sentence #1: ____

____ . }

Textual Evidence

-

-

Commentary/Analysis

-

{ Topic Sentence #2: _________________ and _____________ are also

similar because ____ . }

Textual Evidence

-

-

Commentary/Analysis

-

-

Evidence Organizer: Response to Literature

Topic Sentence #3: While ___________ and __________ are similar because
___________________________, they are different in several ways.

Textual Evidence

-
-
-

Commentary/Analysis

-
-
-

Completed Writing Frame: Response to Literature

Trickster Characters
(An interesting title for your response to literature)

INTRODUCTION

Trickster tales are filled with many interesting characters. In the story

"The Fox and the Crow" , Fox is interesting because
(identify first story)   (identify first character)

he is clever . In contrast, in the story "How Coyote
(identify one reason why this character is interesting)   (identify second story)

Turned Gray" , Coyote is interesting because
(identify second story)   (identify second character)

he is so vain . Fox and Coyote are
(identify reason why this character is interesting)   (identify first character)   (identify second character)

similar because they are both sly and sneaky but different
(identify first way they are similar)   (identify second way they are similar)

because Fox uses his head to get what he wants and Coyote is just copying
(identify one reason for each character why they are different)

the bird to make himself look pretty. .

BODY

Both Fox and Coyote are similar because
(identify first character)   (identify second character)

they are both sneaky . For example, Fox
(include first way characters are similar)   (identify first character)

sees the cheese he likes . Later, Crow drops the cheese and Fox gets his cheese. .
(provide example)   (explain what happens)

Like Fox , Coyote is real sneaky. He spies on the bird. He
(identify character #1)   (identify second character)   (explain how second character is similar to first character)

decides to jump in the lake . Later, Coyote is blue and so proud of himself that he
(explain what happens)

falls to the ground and turns dark .
(explain what happens)

BODY

Fox and Coyote are also similar because
(identify first character)   (identify second character)

Completed Writing Frame: Response to Literature

BODY

they get what they want
(include second way characters are similar)

Fox gets his yummy cheese and he was happy
(Include examples that show this similarity)

and gives Crow advise for the cheese. Coyote gets what he wants too. At first he wants

to be blue. He falls on the ground. He turns the color of the dirt. He decides that this is

good thing. Because he could become a better trickster if he is not blue .

While ____Fox____ and ____Coyote____ are similar, there are also important
(identify first character)   (identify second character)

differences between these two characters. For example, ____Fox____
(identify first character)

talks to crow he tells him nice things to get the cheese. He is hungry and needed the
(identify differences between first character and second character)

cheese. He gets his way, but he is honest with Crow. He tells him not to trust a flaturer .

____Coyote____, on the other hand, ____is very selfish and proud.
(identify second character)   (include examples that show differences)

He wants to be pretty like the blue bird, but when he turns blue he dances around. He

shouldn't do that because he falls down and turns gray anyway his selfishness was his

biggest problem. People shouldn't be selfish .

CONCLUSION

Tricksters, like ____Fox____ and ____Coyote____ , are ____
(identify first character)   (identify second character)

interesting, sly, and sneeky . However, Fox is smart and honest. He is
(restate the similarities using different words)

just hungry. Coyote is sly. But he was too proud of himself . In the end, both
(tell how these characters are different and how it affects the stories)

Fox and Coyote are happy because they get what they whanted. There tricks worked .
(explain what happens to each in the end)

Idea Workshop: Response to Literature

Read your response to literature aloud to your reviewer. Then ask your reviewer the following question. Write your reviewer's response below.

What did you like best about my response to literature?

____

____

Directions: Give your response to literature and your Writer's Notebook to your partner. Answer the following questions about your partner's response to literature.

{ REVIEWER: _________________________ }

1. How would you summarize my response to literature?

____

____

____

2. What is my controlling idea?

____

____

____

3. What evidence supports my controlling idea?

____

____

____

Idea Workshop: Response to Literature

4. Is there any evidence that needs to be taken out because it isn't important or it isn't from the text? If so, write this evidence below.

5. What could I do to improve my response to literature?

Editor's Workshop: Response to Literature

Directions: Read each sentence of your partner's response to literature paper. Circle short, related sentences in the paper. Use participial phrases to connect them. Number the sentence on your partner's response to literature paper. Write the corrections below next to the same number.

{ **REVIEWER:** _________________________________ }

Edited Sentences

1. ____
   ____

2. ____
   ____

3. ____
   ____

4. ____
   ____

5. ____
   ____

6. ____
   ____

Scoring Rubric: Response to Literature

Rate the following categories from your Response to Literature on a scale of 1 through 4, with 4 being the most effective and 1 being ineffective. A rating of 0 means you did not attempt to include this feature in your Response to Literature.

Feature	Rating
I established a controlling idea clearly.	0 1 2 3 4
I developed my topic with relevant evidence.	0 1 2 3 4
I showed an understanding of the text.	0 1 2 3 4
I organized my writing with a strong introduction, body, and conclusion.	0 1 2 3 4
I included a variety of sentence types.	0 1 2 3 4
I corrected my writing for grammar, spelling, and punctuation.	0 1 2 3 4

When I write a response to literature in the future, I plan to…

☐ revisit the response to literature prompt while I'm writing.

☐ make sure that my response to literature clearly establishes a controlling idea.

☐ provide relevant evidence.

☐ show an understanding of the text.

☐ effectively organize the writing.

☐ include a variety of sentence types.

☐ edit more carefully for correct grammar, spelling, and punctuation.

☐ _______________________________

Writing Prompt: Response to Literature

Think About It

Trickster tales are told around the world. For the audience, the themes of these tales include a message, a lesson about life or a belief about people and their actions. These themes are often developed through the character's actions. Think about two tales you have read, and consider the similarities and differences between the themes of the stories.

Write About It

Write a response to literature in which you compare and contrast the themes of two trickster tales. Develop a thoughtful interpretation of each theme, and explain how the characters' motives and actions help to develop the theme. Be sure to include both the similarities and differences between the themes of these two stories. Organize your writing effectively, with a clear introduction, body, and conclusion. Support your ideas with evidence from the text.

{ RESPONSE TO LITERATURE CHECKLIST }

- ☐ Read the prompt carefully and respond to all parts of the prompt.
- ☐ Develop a thoughtful interpretation.
- ☐ Organize your writing with a strong introduction, body, and conclusion.
- ☐ Use specific details and examples from the reading selection to show your understanding of the main ideas
- ☐ Use words that are appropriate to your audience and purpose.
- ☐ Check for mistakes in grammar, spelling, and punctuation.

Topic Toss: Response to Literature

$\{$ Themes of Trickster Tales $\}$

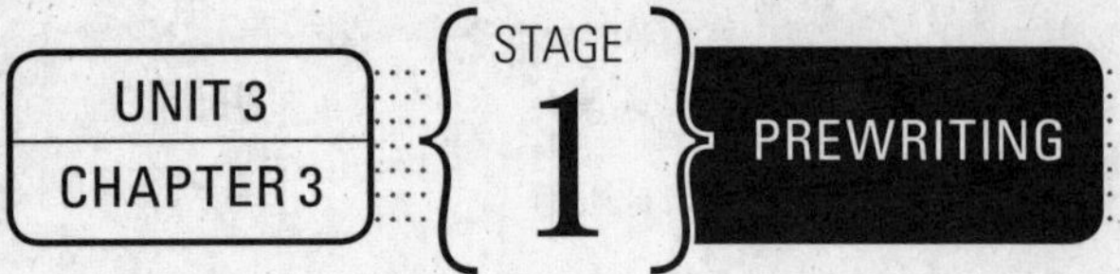

Contrasting Themes Log

Text: ____

{ **THEME #1** }

{ **THEME #2** }

{ **Similarities Between Themes Because the Characters:** }

Differences Between Characters with Regard to:

← ⋯⋯ **MOTIVES** ⋯⋯ →

← ⋯⋯ **ACTIONS** ⋯⋯ →

Evidence Organizer: Response to Literature

Controlling Idea: The themes of _________________________ and _________________________ are similar because _________________________ ____ but different because ____.

{ Topic Sentence 1: The themes from the two stories are similar because ____. }

Textual Evidence

-
-
-

Commentary/Analysis

-
-

{ Topic Sentence 2: One difference between the themes is that ____. }

Textual Evidence

-
-
-

Commentary Analysis

-
-
-

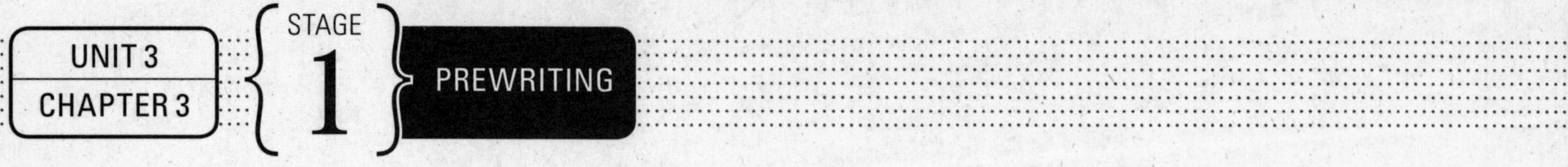

Topic Sentence 3: While __________,
__________.

Textual Evidence

-
-
-

Commentary/Analysis

-
-
-

Completed Writing Frame: Response to Literature

Fox and Badger

(a creative title that relates to your topic)

INTRODUCTION

The Fox and the Crow is about how you should be careful about people who always tell you how nice you are. How Badger tricked the Monster is about how important it is to be as honest as you can. Both of these stories teach us how to be better people be careful about other people too.

(controlling idea)

BODY

Fox and the Badger are both trickey characters. They are the same because they have to trick the other one so they get what they want. Fox can trick people by telling him how nice he looks like Crow and then get the cheese they like. Badger tricked the monster because he told him the truth about being scared of money. The monster gave him money anyway. Monster tried to hurt and scare. Crow got mad and cawed, and that is how their both tricky.

BODY

They are smart. Badger wanted to go to school and help his mother, and fox wanted

the cheese he liked. They had to be tricky and get what they wanted. Only crow did not

talk to fox like monster did. Fox and Badger had to be smart alot of the time in both

stories.

BODY

If your honest then you get what you want was what Badger and the Monster was

about. It is different than the Fox story because Fox told Crow how nice he was and got

the cheese.

CONCLUSION

I think Badger is better than Fox because he had to save his life and tell the Monster

that he was scared of money. That was smart because Monster was going to eat him

and Badger was scared. All Fox did was tell the Crow how nice he was then he got some

cheese. I like Badger better.

Idea Workshop: Response to Literature

Read your response to literature aloud to your reviewer. Then ask your reviewer the following question. Write your reviewer's response below.

What did you like most about my response to literature?

____

____

____

Now give your response to literature and your Writer's Notebook to your reviewer.

{ REVIEWER: } ____

1. How would you summarize my response to literature?

____

____

____

____

2. What is my controlling idea?

____

____

3. What evidence supports my controlling idea?

____

____

____

Idea Workshop: Response to Literature

4. Is there any evidence that need to be taken out because it is not important or from the text? If so, write the evidence below.

5. What could I do to improve my response to literature?

Editor's Workshop: Response to Literature

Read each sentence in your partner's response to literature. Find independent clauses in your partner's response to literature that could be combined by rewriting one as a dependent clause of the other independent clause. Number the sentences on your response to literature. Write the corrections below.

REVIEWER: _______________________

Edited Sentences

1. ____

    ____

2. ____

    ____

3. ____

    ____

4. ____

    ____

5. ____

    ____

6. ____

    ____

Scoring Rubric: Response to Literature

Rate the following categories from your response to literature on a scale of 1 through 4, with 4 being the most effective and 1 being ineffective. A rating of 0 means you did not attempt to include this feature in your response to literature.

Feature	Rating
I established a controlling idea clearly.	0 1 2 3 4
I developed my topic with important evidence.	0 1 2 3 4
I showed an understanding of the text.	0 1 2 3 4
I organized my writing with a strong introduction, body, and conclusion.	0 1 2 3 4
I included a variety of sentence types.	0 1 2 3 4
I corrected my writing for grammar, spelling, and punctuation.	0 1 2 3 4

When I write a response to literature in the future, I plan to…

- ☐ revisit the response to literature prompt while I'm writing.
- ☐ make sure that my response to literature clearly establishes a controlling idea.
- ☐ provide important evidence.
- ☐ show an understanding of the text.
- ☐ effectively organize the writing.
- ☐ include a variety of sentence types.
- ☐ edit more carefully for correct grammar, spelling, and punctuation.
- ☐ ____

Writing Prompt: Research Report

Think About It

In this unit, you are reading about storms and how to stay safe during storms. You have just learned about thunderstorms. Imagine that you are a park ranger who has been asked to write a research report for visitors to your park. What makes thunderstorms dangerous? Think about the warning signs and dangers of thunderstorms.

Write About It

Write a research report for *Camping Journal* to inform campers of the dangers of thunderstorms. Organize your writing with a strong introduction, body, and conclusion. Establish a controlling idea and develop topic sentences to support your topic. Be sure to include important supporting details from more than one source.

{ **RESEARCH REPORT CHECKLIST** }

☐ Read the prompt carefully and address all parts of the prompt.

☐ Organize your writing with a strong introduction, body, and conclusion.

☐ Develop a controlling idea or topic.

☐ Use specific details and examples to fully support your ideas.

☐ Include information from more than one source.

☐ Use words that are appropriate to your audience and purpose.

Topic Toss: Research Report

{ Dangers of Thunderstorms }

Information Log

Text: ____

{ Subject }   { Notes }

On-the-Surface
who, where, when, and what happened

Under-the-Surface
how, why, would, could, and should

Reflection

____

____

____

Evidence Organizer

Topic: ____

Controlling Idea: People ____________________ should ____________________

____________________, ____________________, and

____________________.

{ Topic Sentence 1: Thunderstorms form when _____________________

_____________________.

Textual Evidence	Source
•	•
•	•
•	•

{ Topic Sentence 2: Thunderstorms are _____________________

_____________________.

Textual Evidence	Source
•	•
•	•
•	•

Evidence Organizer

Topic Sentence 3: Campers need to know _______________________

_______________________.

Textual Evidence

-
-
-

Source

-
-
-

Completed Writing Frame: Research Report

"Dangerous Thunderstorms"

(a creative title that relates to your topic)

INTRODUCTION

Springtime can be a ___dangerous___ time for campers because
(record adjective)

___its thunderstorn season___ . Thunderstorms are ___a natural disaster___ .
(explain choice of adjective) (describe thunderstorm)

People ___planning a camping trip___ should ___be aware of how they form___ ,
(record dependent clause) (record topic 1)

___what makes them dangerous___ , and ___how to now when they are coming___ .
(record topic 2) (record topic 3)

BODY

Thunderstorms form when ___clouds get really heavy with rain___ . According to
(explain how thunderstorms form)

___an article in the encyclpeda___ , " ___A thunderstorm is a from of weather___
(identify source #1) (record evidence 1)

_______________________________________ ." This causes

___rain to fall___ . As a result, ___The wind pushes the rain down___ .
(explain what happens next) (explain conclusion)

Thunderstorms, ___sometimes___ , ___become dangerous when___
(include appositive describing thunderstorms) (record fact)

BODY

___there is lightning___ . They can cause ___forest fires___ ,
(explain consequences)

or ___floods___ . In addition, they can cause
(explain consequences)

Completed Writing Frame: Research Report

BODY

lightening and _hale_ .
(explain consequences)   (explain consequences)

Campers _who care about the envirment need to know this stuff_ .
(record effects)

Therefore, _people should stay inside there house_
(explain conclusion)

in a thunderstorm (_Whitley_).
(identify source)

Campers need to know _the warning of thunderstorms_ .
(complete topic sentence)

In Radar it states _"_ _storms can occur unexpectedly_ _"_
(identify source 3)   (record evidence 3)

In addition, scientists _watch the radar and satellite for changes in the atmosphere_ .
(record evidence 3)

Knowing this will help campers _stay safe in always_ .
(explain conclusion)

CONCLUSION

Campers should _learn all they can about camping_ .
(write statement about understanding thunderstorms)

As long as _campers learn a lot about camping, they will be safe_ .
(include explanation/under-the-surface reflection)

Being safe _is really important to campers._
(include explanation)

This information could save your life.

Idea Workshop: Research Report

Give your research report and your Writer's Notebook to your reviewer. Answer the following questions about your reviewer's research report. Write your reviewer's response below.

What did you like most about my research report?

____

____

____

Read your partner's research report, then write your answers to the questions below.

{ **REVIEWER:** _______________________ }

1. In one sentence, summarize my research report.

____

____

____

2. What are my topic sentences?

____

____

____

____

3. What evidence did I include to support my controlling idea?

____

____

____

Idea Workshop: Research Report

4. Are there any details that need to be taken out? What are they?

5. What sources did I use?

6. What could I do to improve my research report?

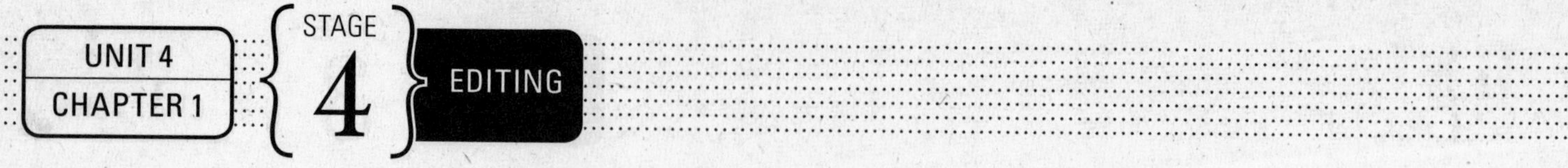

Editor's Workshop: Research Report

Directions: Read each sentence in your partner's research report. Find sentences with titles, quotes, and citations that are incorrectly written or missing. Number the sentences on your partner's report. Write the corrections below.

{ REVIEWER: _______________________ }

Edited Sentences

1. ____

____

2. ____

____

3. ____

____

4. ____

____

5. ____

____

6. ____

____

Scoring Rubric: Research Report

Rate the following categories from your research report on a scale of 1 through 4, with 4 being the most effective and 1 being ineffective. A rating of 0 means you did not attempt to include this feature in your research report.

Feature	Rating				
I clearly established a controlling idea.	0	1	2	3	4
I developed my topic with relevant evidence and used supporting details from more than one source.	0	1	2	3	4
I organized my writing with a strong introduction, body, and conclusion.	0	1	2	3	4
I used words that are appropriate to my audience and purpose.	0	1	2	3	4
I included a variety of sentence types.	0	1	2	3	4
I corrected my writing for grammar, spelling, and punctuation.	0	1	2	3	4

When I write a research report in the future, I plan to...

- ☐ revisit the research report prompt while I'm writing.
- ☐ make sure that my research report clearly establishes a controlling idea.
- ☐ provide relevant evidence and supporting details from several sources.
- ☐ effectively organize the writing.
- ☐ use words that are appropriate for the audience and purpose.
- ☐ include a variety of sentence types.
- ☐ edit more carefully for correct grammar, spelling, and punctuation.
- ☐ ____

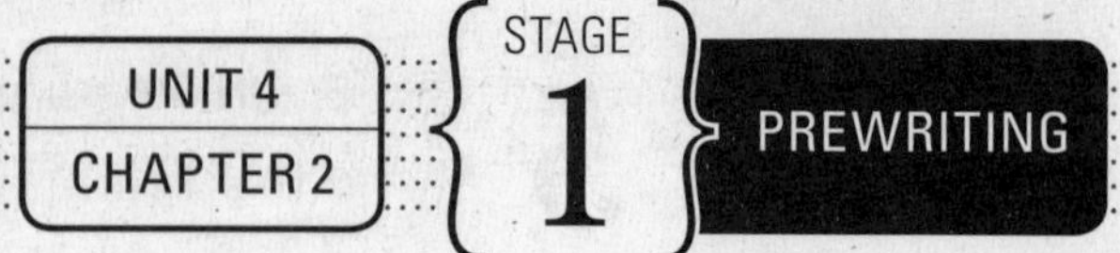

Writing Prompt: Research Report

Think About It

Tornadoes are a type of violent storm in certain parts of the United States. Because these storms can be very dangerous, travelers to Tornado Alley need to be aware of potential tornadoes. Using the information provided in "Twister Chasers" and "Tornado Alley," write a report for tourists informing them of the dangers of tornadoes. Think about what tourists need to know prior to visiting Tornado Alley, including the dangers of tornadoes and safety measures.

Write About It

Write a research report for travelers about the dangers of tornadoes. Organize your writing with a strong introduction, body, and conclusion. Establish a controlling idea and develop topic sentences to support your topic. Be sure to include important supporting details from more than one source.

{ **RESEARCH REPORT CHECKLIST** }

- ☐ Read the prompt carefully and respond to all parts of the prompt.
- ☐ Organize your writing with a strong introduction, body, and conclusion.
- ☐ Develop a controlling idea or topic.
- ☐ Use specific details and examples to fully support your ideas.
- ☐ Include information from more than one source.
- ☐ Use words that are appropriate to your audience and purpose.
- ☐ Check for errors in grammar, spelling, and punctuation.

Topic Toss: Research Report

{ Dangers of Tornadoes }

Information Filter

Text: ____

{ keep information that meets the following criteria }   { leave out information that meets the following criteria }

- important facts/details
- information that relates to the prompt
- safety measures people need to take
- causes/effects of tornadoes

- unimportant facts/details
- repeated information
- opinions
- untrue information

{ include in my research report }   { leave out of my research report }

{ one sentence summary of information }

Evidence Organizer: Research Report

Topic: Tornado dangers and safety measures

Controlling Idea: Tornadoes are important because they are _________________,
(reason #1)

_________________ , and _________________ .
(reason #2)   (reason #3)

Topic Sentence 1: The most important thing about tornadoes is

_________________ .
(reason #1)

Textual Evidence   **Source**

-
-
-

Topic Sentence 2: Another important thing about tornadoes is

_________________ .
(reason #2)

Textual Evidence   **Source**

-
-
-

Evidence Organizer: Research Report

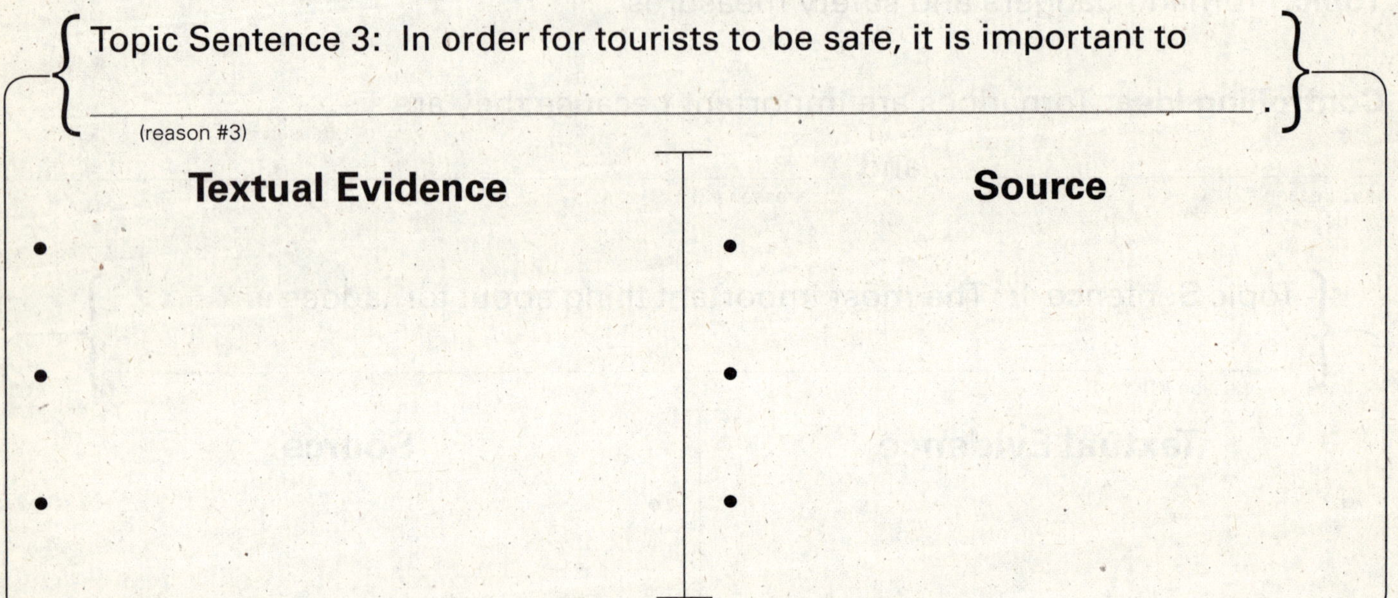

Topic Sentence 3: In order for tourists to be safe, it is important to ____________________.

(reason #3)

Textual Evidence

-
-
-

Source

-
-
-

Completed Writing Frame: Research Report

Tornadoes
(an interesting title for your research report)

INTRODUCTION

Tornadoes are _important_ (record adjective) and _interesting_ (record adjective) storms. Most tornadoes

are _in places like Texas and flat places, but not in California_ (summarize where or what tornadoes are) . Travelers to Tornado

Alley need to know _that tornados can happen at anytime_ (explain what visitors need to know) . Tornadoes are important

because _are very windy_ (record reason #1) , _destroy so much stuff_ (record reason #2) , and _they are hard to find_ (record reason #3) .

BODY

The most important thing about tornadoes is they are fast and windy
(record topic sentence #1)

First, _they are very fast_ (record evidence) .

Also (select transition: Also/Additionally/This includes) , _the wind blows in circles_ (record evidence) .

As _the wind blows in a circle_ (connect to last idea) , _it goes faster and faster_ (record evidence) .

According to _twister chasers_ (source) , _"As soon as a twister hits, it picks up dirt."_ (record quotation)

Because of this, _they are called funnel clouds_ (record conclusion) .

BODY

Another important thing about tornadoes is they destroy so much stuff
(record topic sentence #2)

For example (select transition: For example/For instance/Sometimes) , _if you got a real nice car, they funnel cloud_ (record evidence)

might just suck up thet car and dump it someplace else and you will lose your car and
(record evidence)

Completed Writing Frame: Research Report

BODY

maybe have to get a new one and who knows
(record evidence)
Sometimes
(select transition: For example/For instance/Sometimes) ,

you have no insurence then you're stuck taking the bus, can't go out with friends
(record evidence) .

According to ___my dad___, "___We should always be prepared for the worst___."
(source)   (record quotation)

This is why ___I am real glad my dad has lots of insurence on are cars___.
(record conclusion)

BODY

In order for tourists to be safe, it is important to know about tornadoes
(record topic sentence #3) .

One guy I red about drives around with a gps looking for the storms and
(record evidence)

then when he finds one, him and his guys take pictures and stuff
(record evidence) .

"___Its the best time of year in the plain area of the United States___,"
(record quotation)

says ___Howard Bluestein___.
(identify name of source)
Sometimes
(select transition: For example/For instance/Sometimes) ,

you are just suppose to avoid them
(record conclusion) .

CONCLUSION

Tornadoes, unlike some other storms, are ___scary___.
(describe tornadoes)

Tornado safety is hard, but can be done
(restate controlling idea) .

Although tornadoes last only for a few minutes, ___they are dangerous___
(describe why it is important to be prepared)

so you need to keep away from them
.

Idea Workshop: Research Report

Read your research report aloud to your reviewer. Then ask your reviewer the following question. Write your reviewer's response below.

What did you like best about my research report?

____

____

____

Give your research report and your Writer's Notebook to your partner. Answer the following questions about your partner's research report.

{ REVIEWER: }

1. In one sentence, summarize my research report.

____

____

____

2. What are my topic sentences?

____

____

____

____

____

____

____

____

Idea Workshop: Research Report

3. What evidence did I include to support my topic sentences?

4. Are there any details that need to be taken out? What are they?

5. What sources did I use?

6. What could I do to improve my research report?

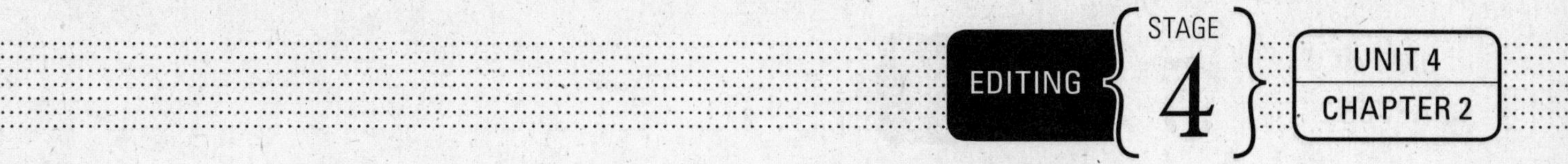

Editor's Workshop: Research Report

Read each sentence in your partner's research report. Find sentences that need to be edited for correctly written complex sentences. Number the sentences on the research report. Write the corrections below.

{ REVIEWER: _______________________ }

Edited Sentences

1. _______________________

2. _______________________

3. _______________________

4. _______________________

5. _______________________

6. _______________________

Scoring Rubric: Research Report

Rate the following categories from your research report on a scale of 1 through 4, with 4 being the most effective and 1 being ineffective. A rating of 0 means you did not attempt to include this feature in your research report.

Feature	Rating				
I clearly established a controlling idea.	0	1	2	3	4
I developed my topic with relevant evidence and used supporting details from more than one source.	0	1	2	3	4
I organized my writing with a strong introduction, body, and conclusion.	0	1	2	3	4
I used words that are appropriate to my audience and purpose.	0	1	2	3	4
I included a variety of sentence types.	0	1	2	3	4
I corrected my writing for grammar, spelling, and punctuation.	0	1	2	3	4

When I write a research report in the future, I plan to…

- ☐ revisit the research report prompt while I'm writing.
- ☐ make sure that my research report clearly establishes a controlling idea.
- ☐ provide relevant evidence and supporting details from several sources.
- ☐ effectively organize the writing.
- ☐ use words that are appropriate for the audience and purpose.
- ☐ include a variety of sentence types.
- ☐ edit more carefully for correct grammar, spelling, and punctuation.
- ☐ ____

Writing Prompt: Research Report

Think About It

The weather channel is running a series about furious winds. You are a researcher who has been asked to write a report comparing two types of furious wind. What are the similarities and differences between these two types of furious wind? Think about their causes, how they can be predicted, how people can prepare for them, and the effects of each type of furious wind.

Write About It

Write a research report for the weather channel about furious winds. Compare and contrast two types of furious wind. Organize your writing with a strong introduction, body, and conclusion. Establish a controlling idea and develop topic sentences to support your topic. Be sure to include important supporting details from more than one source.

{ **RESEARCH REPORT CHECKLIST** }

- ☐ Read the prompt carefully and address all parts of the prompt.
- ☐ Organize your writing with a strong introduction, body, and conclusion.
- ☐ Develop a controlling idea or topic.
- ☐ Include specific details and examples from more than one source.
- ☐ Use words that are appropriate to your audience and purpose.
- ☐ Check for errors in grammar, spelling, and punctuation.

Topic Toss: Research Report

{ Describe the different furious winds }

Contrasting Concepts Log

{ CONCEPT #1 }

{ CONCEPT #2 }

{ Similarities Between Concepts }

Differences Between Concepts With Regard To:

← - - - CAUSES - - - →

← - - - PREDICTING - - - →

← - PREPARING FOR - →

← - - - EFFECTS - - - →

Evidence Organizer: Research Report

Topic: What are the similarities and differences between two furious winds?

Controlling Idea: While _______________ and _______________ are different types of furious wind, there are _______________ in _______________,

_______________, and _______________.

Topic Sentence 1: _______________

_______________.

Evidence

Source

-
-
-

Topic Sentence 2: _______________

_______________.

Evidence

Source

-
-
-

Evidence Organizer: Research Report

{ Topic Sentence 3: _______________________________________

_______________________________________. }

Evidence

-
-
-

Source

-
-
-

Completed Writing Frame: Research Report

Furious Winds

(a creative title for your research report)

INTRODUCTION

There are natural disasters in our world today. Tornadoes and hurricanes are big

storms that reck buildings and homes and kill people. While tornadoes and hurricanes

(controlling idea)

have many things that are the same, the cause damage, and predicting are different.

BODY

Tornadoes start on the land, and tropical storms start over the ocean. Tornadoes

happen when cold air comes in and meets warm air. According to "Hurricanes,"

"a hurricane is a tropcal storm that froms over warm water in the shape of a spiral.

Tornadoes too. When a hurricane hits land, you are supposed to be in a high spot, so you

are not flooded out. If you were in a tornado you could hide in your basement to stay safe

but that isn't a good idea in a hurricane, because then you would drown.

BODY

Tornadoes and hurricanes have winds that can wreck a lot of things. If they are not

spinning too fast then you might only have some trees fall down but if the wind is really

Completed Writing Frame: Research Report

really strong, then the winds can rip apart big buildings and boats and cars to. There was

a hurricane in Florida named Charley that made people evacuate the city for because

they had lots of time to get out and some peple had to leave there dogs and stuff behind.

I saw the pitures of all the dogs and stuff that didnt have homes or places to stay

because of the hurricane.

Tornados and hurricanes have people that track storms. Storm chasers are peple that

go out and try to get information using computers and maps and other things. Hurricane

hunter is the name for peple that like to fly into the middle of the hurricane to get

important information to warn peple. Both of thier jobs are hard, but they help people.

Tornadoes and hurricanes are natural disasters that cause lots of damage. They are

similar and different in many ways. Tornadoes are winds over land and hurricanes are

storms that start over water.

Idea Workshop: Research Report

Read your research report aloud to your reviewer. Then ask your reviewer the following question. Write your reviewer's response below.

What did you like best about my research report?

____

____

Give your research report and your Writer's Notebook to your partner. Answer the following questions about your partner's research report.

{ **REVIEWER:**

1. In one sentence, summarize my research report.

____

____

____

2. What are my topic sentences?

____

____

____

____

____

____

____

Idea Workshop: Research Report

3. What evidence did I include to support my controlling idea?

4. Are there any details that need to be taken out? What are they?

5. What sources did I use?

6. What could I do to improve my research report?

Editor's Workshop: Research Report

Read each sentence in your partner's research report. Find sentences that need to be edited for correctly written compound and complex sentences. Number the sentences on the research report. Write the corrections below.

{ REVIEWER: } ________________________________

Edited Sentences

1. ____

____

2. ____

____

3. ____

____

4. ____

____

5. ____

____

6. ____

____

Scoring Rubric: Research Report

Rate the following categories from your research report on a scale of 1 through 4, with 4 being the most effective and 1 being ineffective. A rating of 0 means you did not attempt to include this feature in your research report.

Feature	Rating
I clearly established a controlling idea.	0 1 2 3 4
I developed my topic with relevant evidence and used supporting details from more than one source.	0 1 2 3 4
I organized my writing with a strong introduction, body, and conclusion.	0 1 2 3 4
I used words that are appropriate to my audience and purpose.	0 1 2 3 4
I included a variety of sentence types.	0 1 2 3 4
I corrected my writing for grammar, spelling, and punctuation.	0 1 2 3 4

When I write a research report in the future, I plan to…

- ☐ revisit the research report prompt while I'm writing.
- ☐ make sure that my research report clearly establishes a controlling idea.
- ☐ provide relevant evidence and supporting details from several sources.
- ☐ effectively organize the writing.
- ☐ use words that are appropriate for the audience and purpose.
- ☐ include a variety of sentence types.
- ☐ edit more carefully for correct grammar, spelling, and punctuation.
- ☐ ____

Score Point 4

The narrative—
- **effectively** addresses the topic;
- clearly shows what happened in the beginning, middle, and end of the event;
- uses concrete sensory details to help the reader picture the setting;
- is written like a story and uses a variety of appropriate narrative strategies (such as character development, dialogue, and vivid descriptive language);
- includes a variety of sentence types and has few or no errors in grammar, spelling, or punctuation.

Score Point 3

The narrative—
- **adequately** addresses the topic;
- shows what happened in the beginning, middle, and end of the event;
- uses some concrete sensory details to help the reader picture the setting;
- is written like a story and uses some narrative strategies (such as character development, dialogue, and vivid descriptive language);
- includes a variety of sentence types and has some errors in grammar, spelling, and punctuation.

Score Point 2

The narrative—
- **minimally** addresses the topic;
- attempts to show what happened in the beginning, middle, and end of the event;
- uses few concrete sensory details that help the reader picture the setting;
- attempts to be written like a story and includes few narrative strategies (such as character development, dialogue, and vivid descriptive language);
- includes little variety of sentence types and has several errors in grammar, spelling, and punctuation that make it hard to read.

Score Point 1

The narrative—
- **ineffectively** addresses the topic;
- is not organized with a clear beginning, middle, and end;
- lacks concrete sensory details to show the setting;
- is not written like a story and lacks narrative strategies (such as character development, dialogue, and vivid descriptive language);
- includes no sentence variety and has many errors in grammar, spelling, and punctuation that make it hard to read.

Score Point 

The writing—
- **effectively** addresses the topic;
- clearly states a position in support of a proposal;
- effectively organizes the writing and provides relevant evidence;
- convincingly addresses the reader's concerns;
- includes a variety of sentence types and has few or no errors in grammar, spelling, or capitalization.

Score Point 

The writing—
- **adequately** addresses the topic;
- states a position in support of a proposal;
- organizes the writing and provides supporting evidence;
- addresses the reader's concerns;
- includes a variety of sentence types and has some errors in grammar, spelling, and capitalization.

Score Point 2

The writing—
- **minimally** addresses the topic;
- attempts to state a position in support of a proposal;
- includes limited organization with some evidence;
- may or may not address the reader's concerns;
- includes little variety in sentence types and has several errors in grammar, spelling, and capitalization that make it hard to read.

Score Point 

The writing—
- **ineffectively** addresses the topic;
- lacks a position in support of a proposal;
- lacks organization and supporting evidence;
- does not address the reader's concerns;
- includes no sentence variety and has many errors in grammar, spelling, and capitalization that make it hard to read.

Score Point

The writing—
- **effectively** addresses the topic;
- clearly establishes a controlling idea;
- clearly demonstrates an understanding of the text and develops a thoughtful interpretation;
- effectively organizes the writing and supports judgments with evidence from the text and prior knowledge;
- includes a variety of sentence types and has few or no errors in grammar, spelling, or punctuation.

Score Point

3

The writing—
- **adequately** addresses the topic;
- establishes a controlling idea;
- demonstrates an understanding of the text and develops an interpretation;
- organizes the writing and supports judgments with evidence from the text and prior knowledge;
- includes a variety of sentence types and has some errors in grammar, spelling, and punctuation.

Score Point

2

The writing—
- **minimally** addresses the topic;
- attempts to establish a controlling idea;
- attempts to demonstrate an understanding of the text and may or may not develop an interpretation;
- attempts to organize the writing, and may or may not support judgments with evidence from the text or prior knowledge;
- includes little variety in sentence types and has several errors in grammar, spelling, and punctuation that make it hard to read.

Score Point

The writing—
- **ineffectively** addresses the topic;
- lacks a controlling idea;
- lacks an understanding of the text and lacks an interpretation;
- does not organize the writing and does not support judgments with evidence from the text or prior knowledge;
- includes no sentence variety and has many errors in grammar, spelling, and punctuation that make it hard to read.

Score Point

The writing—
- **effectively** addresses the topic;
- clearly establishes a controlling idea or topic;
- effectively develops the topic with relevant facts, details, and examples from more than one source;
- effectively organizes the writing, including a strong introduction, body, and conclusion;
- includes a variety of sentence types and has few or no errors in grammar, spelling, or punctuation.

Score Point

3

The writing—
- **adequately** addresses the topic;
- establishes a controlling idea or topic;
- develops the topic with facts, details, and examples from more than one source;
- organizes the writing, including an introduction, body, and conclusion;
- includes a variety of sentence types and has some errors in grammar, spelling, and punctuation.

Score Point

2

The writing—
- **minimally** addresses the topic;
- attempts to establish a controlling idea or topic;
- attempts to develop the topic with limited facts, details, and examples;
- attempts to organize the writing, including an introduction, body, and conclusion;
- includes little variety in sentence types and has several errors in grammar, spelling, and punctuation that make it hard to read.

Score Point

The writing—
- **ineffectively** addresses the topic;
- lacks a controlling idea or topic;
- may or may not include simple facts, details, and examples;
- does not organize the writing;
- includes no sentence variety and has many errors in grammar, spelling, and punctuation that make it hard to read.

{a}

a lot (adj.) many, plenty, masses, loads, heaps, several, numerous, tremendous, various, multitudinous, multifarious, frequent, manifold. (ANT.) few, meager, scanty, infrequent.

{b}

bad (adj.) dreadful, unfavorable, wrong, faulty, improper, tainted, defective, evil, wicked, corrupt, immoral, unscrupulous, ruthless, merciless, cruel, awful, terrible, appalling, shocking, ghastly, horrific, dire, unpleasant, disobedient, defiant, troublesome, wayward, mischievous, unruly, rude, rotten, decayed, putrid, stale, rancid. (ANT.) good, honorable, moral, excellent.

beautiful (adj.) gorgeous, stunning, pretty, fair, charming, striking, attractive, handsome, lovely, exquisite, magnificent. (ANT.) ugly, unattractive, repulsive, hideous, foul, homely, nasty, unpleasant, unsightly, repugnant.

big (adj.) large, huge, gigantic, vast, bulky, immense, massive, colossal, majestic, monstrous, enormous, tremendous. (ANT.) small, little, tiny, immature, petite.

brave (adj.) bold, courageous, intrepid, fearless, undaunted, daring, gallant, valorous, adventurous, valiant, heroic, magnanimous. (ANT.) cowardly, weak, cringing, timid, fearful, craven.

but (conj.) nevertheless, however, yet, except, though, although.

{c}

calm (adj./v.) peaceful, still, serene, relaxed, appease, lull, quiet, soothe, composed, tranquil, dispassionate. (ANT.) agitated, tempestuous, disturbed, turmoil, inflame.

{d}

dangerous (adj.) unsafe, treacherous, risky, perilous, precarious, threatening, hazardous. (ANT.) safe, secure, harmless, immune.

dream (n./v.) fantasy, wish, hope, vision, illusion, goal, trance, reverie, imagine, envision, visualize, fantasize, aspiration. (ANT.) reality, actuality, truth.

{e}

easy (adj.) effortless, simple, trouble-free, straightforward, uncomplicated. (ANT.) difficult, hard, tough, arduous, challenging, complicated, complex, intricate.

excited (adj.) eager, thrilled, energized, agitated, invigorated. (ANT.) calm, relaxed, bored, tired.

{f}

fast (adj.) quick, fleet, speedy, rapid, brisk, swift, hasty, prompt, expeditious, rushed. (ANT.) slow, sluggish, unhurried, deliberate, leisurely, dawdling, easygoing, thorough.

foolish (adj.) silly, senseless, idiotic, unwise, imprudent, thoughtless, irrational. (ANT.) wise, intelligent, clever, sensible, prudent, reasonable, brilliant.

{g}

go (v.) leave, flee, depart, exit, move, quit, travel, proceed, progress, vanish. (ANT.) arrive, stay, stand, come, enter.

good (adj.) valid, fine, honorable, excellent, worthy, decent, moral, virtuous, conscientious, noble, marvelous, magnificent, adequate, pleasant, satisfactory, agreeable, humane, kind, fair, genial. (ANT.) bad, awful, terrible, imperfect, vicious, dreadful, undesirable, unkind, evil.

{h}

happy (adj.) joyous, cheerful, content, pleased, overjoyed, merry, satisfied, glad, blissful, exultant, ecstatic, delighted, optimistic, cheery, jovial, fortunate. (ANT.) sad, distressed, glum, sullen, gloomy, morose, sorrowful, miserable, depressed.

hard (adj.) difficult, arduous, rigid, burdensome, complicated, puzzling, tough, durable, inflexible, firm. (ANT.) fluid, easy, simple, effortless, gentle, tender, soft, flexible, smooth, lenient.

hit (v.) strike, collide, knock, pound, pummel, punch, thump, slap, beat, smack, batter, knock, whack, bang, cuff, rap.

{i}

important (adj.) significant, critical, momentous, grave, pressing, vital, central, essential, pivotal, crucial, focal, relevant, prominent, imperative, principal, precious, valuable, worthy, notable, illustrious. (ANT.) insignificant, unimportant, trifling, petty, trivial, minor, irrelevant, secondary.

interested (adj.) engaged, captivated, enthralled, immersed, fascinated, attracted, motivated, engrossed, absorbed. (ANT.) bored, uninterested, weary.

{k}

kid (n.) child, toddler, teenager, teen, adolescent, youngster. (ANT.) adult, elder.

{l}

leave (v.) depart, go, evacuate, flee, scatter, retire, desert, abandon, withdraw, relinquish, quit, forsake, renounce, escape, abscond, disappear. (ANT.) stay, come, arrive, abide, remain.

like (v.) enjoy, fancy, esteem, adore, love, admire, care for, prefer, cherish. (ANT.) dislike, disapprove, detest, loathe, abhor.

look (n./v.) gaze, stare, witness, watch, peer, examine, glance, scan, glare, view, glimpse, peep, peek. (ANT.) overlook, avert, miss, hide.

lose (v.) misplace, fail, sacrifice, forfeit, mislay, vanish, surrender. (ANT.) find, discover, locate, succeed, win.

{m}

mad (adj.) angry, furious, livid, raging, irate, fierce, disgruntled, indignant, infuriated, fuming, exasperated, delirious, provoked, incensed, insane, uncontrollable, frenzied, illogical, ludicrous, preposterous, ridiculous, foolish, nutty. (ANT.) pleased, happy, cheerful, content, delighted, thrilled, sane, rational, lucid, sensible, calm.

mean (adj.) nasty, unkind, hostile, evil, cruel, merciless, vicious, heartless, ruthless, harsh, vindictive, brutal, pitiless, spiteful, callous, uncaring, malicious, despicable, cantankerous, unpleasant. (ANT.) compassionate, dignified, sympathetic, empathetic, concerned, kind, kindhearted, considerate, caring, benevolent.

{n}

nice (adj.) pleasing, pleasant, agreeable, thoughtful, friendly, good, fine, enjoyable, gratifying, cordial, polite, compassionate, dignified, sympathetic, empathetic, concerned, kind, kindhearted, considerate, caring, benevolent. (ANT.) unpleasant, nasty, unkind, evil, cruel, merciless, vicious, heartless, ruthless, harsh, vindictive, brutal, pitiless, spiteful, callous, careless, thoughtless, malicious, despicable.

{o}

OK (adj.) reasonable, acceptable, satisfactory, passable, tolerable. (ANT.) unsatisfactory, inadequate, poor, insufficient, disappointing, unacceptable, substandard.

{p}

pretty (adj.) attractive, beautiful, dazzling, cute, appealing, charming, handsome, lovely, fair, elegant. (ANT.) unattractive, hideous, repulsive, foul, unsightly, homely, plain.

problem (n.) difficulty, trouble, crisis, dilemma, predicament, quandary, glitch, hindrance, obstruction, burden, obstacle, conundrum, challenge.

proud (adj.) gratified, haughty, arrogant, conceited, pompous, overbearing, stately, vain, self-righteous, disdainful, overconfident, bigheaded, egotistical. (ANT.) humble, modest, unassuming, meek, ashamed, lowly.

{r}

ran (v.) sprinted, fled, jogged, loped, scuttled, scampered, darted, dashed, scurried, rushed, hurried, raced.

really (adv.) truly, actually, honestly, thoroughly, genuinely, undoubtedly, positively, sincerely, exceedingly, especially, very. (ANT.) possibly, doubtfully, questionably.

{s}

sad (adj.) gloomy, despairing, dejected, lamenting, despondent, solemn, disconsolate, doleful, miserable, sorrowful,

depressed, cheerless, distressed,
anguished, heartbreaking, poignant. (ANT.)
cheerful, happy, glad, jolly, joyful, merry,
positive, jovial, lively.

said (v.) spoke, uttered, articulated, declared,
announced, pronounced, stated, cried,
shouted, verbalized, answered, replied,
exclaimed, voiced, vocalized, conversed,
expressed, revealed, whispered.

saw (v.) observed, perceived, distinguished,
noticed, witnessed, spotted, took a glimpse.

scared (adj.) afraid, frightened,
apprehensive, terrified, fearful,
fainthearted, timid, petrified. (ANT.)
fearless, intrepid, brave, undaunted,
courageous, bold, composed, sanguine,
unafraid, daring, valiant.

scary (adj.) daunting, ghastly, horrifying,
frightening, appalling, creepy, chilling,
terrifying, forbidding, bloodcurdling,
intimidating, alarming, startling, menacing.
(ANT.) calming, comforting, restful, gentle,
peaceful, relaxing.

slow (adj.) sluggish, gradual, delaying,
unhurried, deliberate, leisurely, dawdling.
(ANT.) fast, quick, swift, speedy, rapid, brisk.

small (adj.) little, minute, tiny, diminutive,
slight, petty, puny, wee, miniature, petite,
undersized, minor, trivial. (ANT.) big,
major, large, huge, gigantic, immense,
enormous, vast.

smart (adj.) clever, astute, skillful, apt,
witty, intelligent, ingenious. (ANT.) foolish,
unskilled, clumsy, bungling, slow.

sneaky (adj.) devious, clandestine, sly,
furtive, surreptitious, cunning, stealthy,
shifty, underhanded, mean, tricky, wily.
(ANT.) straightforward, honest, blatant,
obvious, transparent, simple.

soft (adj.) gentle, lenient, mellow,
yielding, squashy, spongy, supple, pliable,
malleable, flexible, bendable. (ANT.) hard,
unyielding, rough, rigid.

special (adj.) particular, individual,
extraordinary, uncommon, unusual,
unique, exceptional, distinctive, peculiar,
different, elite. (ANT.) average, broad,
general, ordinary, common, regular.

strong (adj.) burly, brawny, muscular,
strapping, sturdy, potent, mighty, resistant,
impregnable, tough, fierce, beefy,
powerful, stalwart. (ANT.) weak, tenuous,
feeble, insipid, brittle, fragile, faint, spindly.

stupid (adj.) unintelligent, dull, half-witted,
obtuse, foolish, witless, idiotic, unwise,
silly, imprudent, ludicrous, ridiculous.
(ANT.) smart, intelligent, sensible, clever,
quick, bright, alert, discerning.

surprised (adj./v.) astonished, astounded,
amazed, flabbergasted, staggered,
stunned, shocked, startled.

{t}

take (v.) seize, obtain, confiscate, receive, acquire, capture, procure, grasp, steal, filch, pocket, appropriate, purloin, grab, pilfer, bear, endure, assume, adopt, tolerate, select, accept. (ANT.) give, provide, offer, present, grant, award, allot, donate.

tell (v.) inform, mention, state, advise, notify, enlighten, convey, impart, report, announce, utter, confess, disclose, declare, divulge, reveal, narrate, relate, recount.

then (adv.) next, afterward, subsequently, followed by, therefore.

tricky (adj.) deceitful, furtive, guileful, insidious, shrewd, sly, stealthy, surreptitious, subtle, underhanded, crafty, cunning, scheming, wily, slippery, difficult, complicated, delicate, risky, thorny, problematic, complex, devious. (ANT.) straight, frank, candid, ingenuous, open, simple.

{u}

ugly (adj.) unattractive, hideous, repulsive, foul, unsightly, homely, plain, revolting, horrid, unpleasant, wicked, nasty. (ANT.) good-looking, nice, friendly, attractive, beautiful, dazzling, cute, appealing, charming, handsome, lovely, fair, elegant.

{v}

very (adv.) extremely, greatly, incredibly, awfully, exceptionally, exceedingly, especially, dreadfully, extraordinarily, enormously, fantastically, vastly.

{w}

walk (v.) step, saunter, stroll, amble, march, stride, pace, hike, toddle, totter, stagger, move, go, tread.

weak (adj.) fragile, feeble, frail, debilitated, delicate, wavering, vulnerable, puny, scrawny, weedy, pathetic, tired, faint, exhausted, limp, flimsy, brittle, pliant, diluted. (ANT.) strong, potent, sturdy, powerful.

weird (adj.) odd, eerie, strange, abnormal, unnatural, bizarre, unconventional, peculiar, uncanny, creepy, unusual. (ANT.) normal, usual, ordinary, typical, customary, common, average, conventional.

win (n./v.) succeed, triumph, prevail, achieve, thrive, obtain, flourish, victory, defeat, gain, earn, accomplish, acquire. (ANT.) lose, fail, miss, forfeit.

worry (n./v.) fret, agonize, concern, apprehension, anxiety, fear, uneasiness, discomfort, nervousness. (ANT.) tranquility, peace, assurance, contentment, placidity.